The Pastoral Associate and the Lay Pastor

The Pastoral Associate and the Lay Pastor

Mary Moisson Chandler

THE LITURGICAL PRESS
Collegeville, Minnesota

To
My husband, Harry, and children, Ann, David and Meg,
who keep the "nest" warm
when I am away from home;
and to
Kathleen, Mary Ann and Susan,
who have taught me to trust my dreams
and who have encouraged me to fly towards them.

Cover photo courtesy of the *Catholic Sentinel,* Portland, Oregon. Cover design by Monica Bokinskie.

1 2 3 4 5 6 7 8 9

Library of Congress Cataloging in Publication Data

Chandler, Mary Moisson, 1945–
The pastoral associate and the lay pastor.

Bibliography: p.
1. Lay ministry—Catholic Church. 2. Catholic Church—Doctrines. I. Title.
BX1920.C52 1986 262′.15 86-10266
ISBN 0-8146-1470-1

Contents

Introduction

Historical Background

"Christ is the light of the nations." This is the short opening sentence of a truly revolutionary document, *Lumen gentium* (Dogmatic Constitution on the Church), promulgated over twenty years ago at the Second Vatican Council. It goes on to say that it is the duty of the Church—sign, instrument, and sacrament of Christ—to proclaim this gospel message to all.

No Catholic doubts that the Church is still commissioned to proclaim the Gospel; it is part of our tradition and understanding of ourselves as Roman Catholics. What *is* new in this document is that it redefines the purpose of the structure of the Church and the role of each of the baptized.

It is a radical departure from the ecclesiology emerging from the Council of Trent in the sixteenth century as a reaction to the Protestant Reformation. Then the Roman Catholic Church could be identified by three characteristics: cult, creed, and code. There was a visible, unified, and uniform worship. There were credal statements which definitively and adequately expressed the faith of its members. There was a recognizable, hierarchical structure with the power to make and enforce rules for its members. The role of the laity was basically to listen to and obey its clergy.

The first chapter of *Lumen gentium,* "The Mystery of the Church," does not begin with the Tridentine clarity of cult, creed, and code as a working definition of Church. Instead it recalls biblical imagery to stir our imaginations and evoke a deeper faith. The Church is a seed, a sheepfold, a cultivated field, the heavenly Jerusalem, our mother, spouse of the Lamb.

The center of the Church is our sharing in the Body and Blood of the Lord in the breaking of the Eucharistic bread. Through this action we are taken into communion with Christ and are made one with one another. Christ is the head of this body, all the baptized together forming the whole. There is a diversity of gifts and functions, but we are *all* formed in his likeness.

This body does have a visible, hierarchical structure, but this organizational component is not to be set apart from or set above the reality of the spiritual community. It would be just as impossible to parcel out the mystery of the incarnate Word into neat packages of God and man, flesh and spirit.

The second chapter of *Lumen gentium*, "The People of God," continues to elaborate on these themes. We are *all* called to be a People of God, *all* called to serve the Lord in holiness. Through baptism, not through ordination, we are consecrated to be a spiritual house and a holy priesthood. Though they differ "essentially and not only in degree," the common priesthood of the faithful and the ministerial or hierarchical priesthood are *ordered to one another*, together constituting the whole priesthood of Jesus Christ.

It is through our baptism that the whole People of God shares in the priestly, prophetic, and kingly office of Christ.

After separate chapters on the hierarchy, laity, and religious, this document reiterates two major themes. In chapter 5, "The Call to Holiness," we are reminded that, no matter what state of life to which we are called, we are called equally to the fullness of Christian life and the perfection of Christian love. Chapter 7, "The Pilgrim Church," reminds us that we are still on a journey to God and the Church herself, and each of us as members will reach the perfection of holiness only in heaven.

What drastic changes in the way we now need to experience ourselves as Church! The Tridentine vision was one which clearly saw (1) ordained ministers who ministered to the faithful; (2) priests and religious solely responsible for evangelization; (3) the religious life totally separate from and superior to the life of the laity.

The new vision of Church wipes out those distinctions. Instead we are all called to share in the priestly, prophetic, and kingly ministry of Jesus Christ. Through baptism we are called to minister to one another and evangelize the nations. While still maintaining a hierarchical structure, we are called to mutual service. Each is called to equal holiness and fullness of service. Each has the *same dignity* conferred through baptism and is called to the *same activity* of proclaiming Christ to the world.

Lumen gentium was and is a truly prophetic document. Speaking God's Word, claiming God's Spirit, it still calls us to a reordering and a revisioning of ourselves as Church. Not a blueprint or even a map, but a statement of faith, it is a call to a journey as the People of God, a journey which will be completed only in heaven.

Over twenty years have passed since the end of Vatican II. What began as prophetic witness about baptismal ministry as the primary call to ministry in the Church has become a practical reality in the lived experience of the Church as the number of priests continues to decline.

In a talk given to a canon law convention in 1983,[1] Fr. James Provost reminded them of what we have already begun to experience: that there is both a critical and growing shortage and a geographical maldistribution of priests. Forty-five percent of the Catholic population lives in Europe and North America, yet we have 73 percent of the priests. He cites a study of the American Church of A.D. 2000 in which conservative estimates show 54 percent *fewer* priests than at the close of Vatican II and 35 percent more Catholics. The number of religious priests (not diocesan clergy) is projected to be 50 percent fewer available for parish ministry at the end of the 1980s than at its beginning. In addition, the average age of clergy is continuing to rise.

That is the "bad news." The good news, Father Provost reminds his audience, is that Vatican II reminded us that every Catholic Christian, through baptism, has both a right *and* an obligation to share in the mission of the Church, and that we can no longer afford the luxury of thinking of the laity's role in ministry as "just filling in for Father." This kind of "Band-Aid" theology can neither get to our deepest wounds nor call forth our deepest gifts.

Understanding "Ministry" in the Church

So, how can we combine these two facts: the growing shortage of priests (and also religious) and the obligation—indeed, the right—of all Catholic Christians to share in the mission of the Church through their baptismal ministry?

The *first step* must be to find a working definition of the word "ministry." The root word "minister" comes from the Latin *minor*, meaning "less." Thus it originally meant "servant," and "ministry" was the service given by the servant.

The *second step* is to be aware that "ministry" and "ministries" belong to the whole Church. They have always been controlled and shaped by the Church. Their nature, variety, and function are totally under the power of the community which continues to rejoice in the power and presence of the Spirit.

The *third step* is to be aware of the changes and developments in ministries which have occurred in the Church in the last two thousand years. That the Church has both formed and changed its ministerial offices can be verified both historically and theologically. A brief survey will show five periods of development in Church ministry:[2]

1. *New Testament times*

Scriptural and patristic writings show both variety and mutation of early Church ministries. The Acts of the Apostles focuses on the "twelve" and their institution of the "seven" to serve the needs of the growing Church. The Corinthian community was based on prophets and teachers. The Pastoral Epistles speak of the "apostolic delegate" and "the elders." Even the titles with which we are all familiar—bishop, priest, and deacon—are ambiguous and overlapping.

Other ministries listed in the New Testament are those of prophet, teacher, administrator, healer, miracle-worker, preacher, speaker in tongues, interpreter. The young Church was very comfortable borrowing freely from its Jewish and Hellenistic backgrounds and adapting or innovating as needs arose in the various communities.

2. *Middle Ages*

This time saw the emergence of the offices of archdeacon and archpriest, the creation of the office of cardinal, and the development of the power and authority of the bishop of Rome. The "minor orders" of porter, exorcist, acolyte, and reader came into being. The major order of subdeacon was created. Chorbishops and deaconesses existed. The diaconate changed from being a permanent ministry to becoming a transitional one leading to priesthood.

3. *Pre-Vatican II*

After the Middle Ages, lay ministries and the ordained ministry of both major and minor orders were gradually absorbed into the priestly office. As one author put it, "This resulted, liturgically, in one hyperactive president of the eucharistic assembly and a mass of passive observers." Inevitably, the priest, with the assistance of a growing number of nuns, took over virtually all of the teaching and shepherding functions of the Church as well.

4. *Vatican II*

As a result of Vatican II, a slow reversal of the process of the priest absorbing all the ministries of the laity was begun. During the Council, the permanent diaconate was restored. Later, in 1972, Paul VI wrote *Ministeria quaedam*, a sort of "sleeper" document, which quietly "tuned" the ministries long associated with priesthood to accord with the spirit of the Council. In this document, the "minor orders" of porter and exorcist were abolished; the "minor orders" of acolyte and lector were reinstituted as lay ministries; the "major order" of subdiaconate was suppressed; and national conferences of bishops were enabled to request the authority to create new ministries that would serve local needs.[3]

Shortly after the Council, pastors could seek permission to install parishioners as Eucharistic ministers. In keeping with the idea of Church as "People of God," new management styles were seen in dioceses and parishes: episcopal vicars were created to aid the bishop in the task of governing; new positions of ministry came into being—director of religious education, parish visitors, etc. Pastoral councils and parish councils came to be.

5. *Post-Vatican II*

The ministries of catechist and cantor began to emerge as clear needs soon after the close of the Council. In the late seventies and early eighties the even more hard-to-define and harder-to-name ministries of parish minister, pastoral associate, and lay pastor began to emerge.

Some Working Definitions: "Ministry" and "Official Ministries"

So we finally get back to the first step, a working definition of "ministry" and "ministries." If we have priests who are ministers, if we are all ministers through baptism, and if we have some emerging specialized ministries with specific responsibilities, can this broad term "ministry" have any meaning left at all? The documents of Vatican II are not very clear about defining ministry. Even the revised Code of Canon Law does not give us a definition of ministry or even clear language about what kinds of people can be called ministers.

For the sake of clarity this booklet will use two terms: "ministry" and "official ministry." "Ministry" arises from baptism as a charism of the Spirit urging us to do Christ's work. Thus we all participate in "ministry." "Official ministry" is a stable function for a spiritual purpose set up by Church law or divine law. It is doing in the name of the community a particular kind of ministry by someone commissioned or designated by the Church to do it.

Summary

We are still in the midst of the explosion created by the documents and vision of Vatican II regarding the ways we are coming to understand ourselves as Church and as ministers. In a short three-year period (1962–1965) the Council began the work of reorienting a Church which had become progressively clerical, hierarchical, and remote. Although it gave us back our baptismal rights and obligations to be a priestly, prophetic, kingly people, it will take decades to explore the implications for ministry in the Church, for ordained and lay, official and baptismal ministry.

There is a call to work and plan together as the needs and charisms of the Church change. There is, however, no need to worry. The Spirit which blessed the early Church with so many ministries and gifts is still present in the Church today. We have Christ's promise of that and he is faithful to his Word.

Notes

1. NOCERCC Convention, Feb. 7–11, 1983, session 3. Talk entitled "Justice in the Church."

2. Outline based on a paper presented by James Coriden, "Ministries for the Future," at the Ninth Annual General Meeting of the Canadian Law Society, Ottawa, Oct. 21–24, 1974.

3. See *Study Text III. Ministries in the Church: Commentary on the Apostolic Letters of Pope Paul VI, "Ministeria Quaedam" and "Ad Pascendum."* (Washington: Publications Office, U.S. Catholic Conference, 1974).

1

Emerging Roles of Parish Minister, Pastoral Associate, and Lay Pastor

Introduction

Today, it is a rare parish in which the laity do not have many roles that, a few years ago, would have been solely the province of the pastor and associate pastor(s). In liturgy, laity are involved as readers and Eucharistic ministers,[1] as song leaders, as catechists, etc. In teaching, they are directing religious education programs, teaching in parish schools, serving as youth ministers, directing adult education, conducting prebaptismal and premarital programs. In the area of pastoral care, they are serving in hospital and bereavement ministry, taking the Eucharist to shut-ins, and counseling. It is hard for anyone not to be aware of the increasing role of the laity in virtually all areas of parish life since Vatican II.

We are all called, through baptism, to assume a part in the priestly, prophetic, and kingly role of Christ. Together with this growth in both awareness and action of many laity is the development of the role of the professional lay minister. This phenomenon comes about because of two interrelated factors.

The first is simply the growing shortage of priests and the impact this has on parish life. The second is more important: an awareness on the part of many laity that they are called to live out a full-time professional ministry in the Church as their vocation.

We are still trying to develop a theology of this new trend—nuns serving in non-traditional roles; single adults seeking careers in Church ministry; married men and women, most with families, seeking to forge new molds into which to pour their baptized lives.

There is no question but that the Church, in order to flourish rather than just survive, needs these new kinds of professionals who are trained in theology, Scripture, liturgy, Church history and tradition, and formed in pastoral competencies. In turn, lay ministers must be educated in order to be able to deal with the myriad problems and have the needed skills to serve the People of God effectively, particularly as the numbers of priests will continue to decline well into the next century.

Dangers, Along with Opportunities

Dangers

Professional lay ministry is emerging so fast that it is very tempting to take on some of the trappings of the old forms of ministry. With no role models, it is easy to develop into a separate professional class, not ordained but not really a part of the laity. It is easy to buy into hierarchicalism and clericalism because we as a Church have not really gotten rid of these evils. It is also easier to want to minister to others rather than to enable people to discover their own ministry.

Opportunities

People no longer need to choose between "religious" and "secular" vocations, but are learning how to combine both. These people serve as a sign, reminders to both pastors and other laity that *all* are called to live holy lives and give service to the Church. They bring to their jobs invaluable personal experience previously unavailable to celibate male priests—experience in marriage, as parents, as women. They call us to recognize and affirm an infinite number of charisms, flowing from the baptism and life experience of each of the faithful. They serve as bridges between priests and laity, between hierarchy and people, as living reminders that what we are as a People of God together is greater than what distinguishes our functions within the Body of Christ.

Parish Minister, Pastoral Associate, Lay Pastor

The first generation of lay people seeking Church ministry in the wake of Vatican II somehow managed to get their own theological education and more often than not create their own jobs. It is through the fruit of their pastoral experience and the eyes of their faith that we are entering the second generation, where it is accepted that lay people are gifted and called, and can function professionally in a still-changing Church.

Both their functions and "naming" are still being shaped and have not yet settled into permanent forms. There is a useful legal saying which applies here: "Practice precedes law." Basically, all that means is that we must look to what is happening *before* we can understand, direct, and regulate it—or even name it. As lay ministries have developed and continue to develop, the *practice* of these emerging ministries on which we can now draw has surfaced one basic distinction in professional lay ministry.

This basic distinction comes about by examining the function of a professional lay minister in a parish. This ministry can take one of two forms. In the first, the professional lay minister can have a specialized job description involving one aspect or area of ministry and limited to a selected part of the parish population (e.g., youth minister, minister to the sick or elderly). In the second, the lay minister has comprehensive involvement in most or all areas of parish life (liturgy, teaching, pastoral work, administration) and relates to the whole parish, not just to a particular group.

The titles we have to "name" these lay ministers are still in a state of flux and have not yet stabilized (remember that "practice precedes law"), but the three titles that seem to be most workable are "parish minister" for one doing specialized ministry and "pastoral associate" or "lay pastor" (sometimes also referred to as "pastoral facilitator" or "pastoral administrator") for one doing comprehensive ministry. A simple definition of each follows. The second group, pastoral associates and lay pastors, is so important to the continued existence of the present form of parish life that they will have a separate chapter devoted to each of them.

Parish Minister

- A pastor calls forth people in the community to exercise a specific pastoral ministry such as liturgical planning, parish visitation, youth ministry, community organization, ministry to the sick, etc.
- The training of a parish minister is in the area of specific responsibility.
- A parish minister may be full-time, part-time, or volunteer.
- A parish minister may seek or may be required to seek certification within this area. Most often parish training or workshops would be sufficient to prepare many of them.

Pastoral Associate

- This title connotes two very important aspects of this job: "pastoral" implies that this person shares in the pastoring responsibilities of the pastor; "associate" calls to shared ministry and responsibility, while recognizing legitimate distinctions between clergy and laity.
- This person is on the parish staff, usually full-time.
- This is a comprehensive ministry, with the pastoral associate having some responsibility for all areas of parish life: liturgy, teaching, pastoral care, administration.

- It is related to the whole parish, not just one part.
- Education is equivalent to that of the pastor, with both having a similar academic background (usually an M.A. or M.Div.), with foundation in canon law, liturgy, theology, Scripture, Church history, pastoral ministry; and pastoral training and/or pastoral experience.
- Hiring is done through the pastor and pastoral council at local level.
- Accountability is to pastor and parish.
- Certification is a possibility as this job emerges.

Lay Pastor[2]

INTRODUCTION

This entirely new position is so complex and so important that it needs a brief introduction here. The 1983 Code of Canon Law has created two new positions in Church life due to the shortage of priests. Canon 517, §2 states that because of such a shortage a diocesan bishop can decide to entrust participation in the exercise of pastoral care of a parish to a lay person.

Language for such persons is in flux, although generally such persons are being called "pastoral administrators." Canon 537, however, mandates that there be in each parish a committee of laity to help with the administrative decisions and responsibilities of a parish. The term "lay pastor" rather than "pastoral administrator" or "pastoral facilitator" is to be preferred because it deals explicitly and exclusively with a lay person called by the bishop to share in the total range of pastoral care in a parish, not just in administration.

Canon 517, §2 also creates the complementary position of priest moderator. In the old code a parish could not exist without a resident priest appointed as pastor by the bishop. This new position of priest moderator allows the bishop to appoint some priests endowed with the faculties of a parish priest who are able to supervise the pastoral care of several parishes without being a resident in each of them. This priest moderator functions as "overseer" of several parishes and works with the lay pastor in each of them.

BRIEF JOB DESCRIPTION

The lay pastor:

- resides in a parish without a resident priest
- is canonically appointed by diocesan bishop
- is responsible to bishop and to parish
- provides pastoral care under direction of a priest moderator and confers with him
- is educated the same as is a pastoral associate
- serves as the visible and symbolic leader of the parish community
- attends to liturgical duties such as weekly and Sunday Communion services, Communion to the sick, preaching, funerals, baptisms
- conducts catechesis for sacraments, other programs
- responds to pastoral emergencies, counseling, liaison with the priest moderator
- is responsible, with finance committee, for administering parish budget and maintaining parish goods

Summary

There is a growing need for professional lay ministers in the Church. Theirs is a distinction in function, not a replacement of baptism, for through it we are all called to serve. There is a need for proper education, training, support, but not to simply modify clericalism or hierarchical structure.

These roles of the professional lay minister are still emerging as they are tested in the crucible of lived parish experience. They are still being formed, defined, and developed. This process will continue for years into the future as the Church works out the practical realities of the call to the prophetic, priestly, and kingly ministry of the People of God.

The three titles of professional ministers which seem most functional right now are as stated above: *parish minister,* with a specific area of responsibility usually to one segment of the parish; *pastoral associate,* with comprehensive ministry in a parish with an ordained pastor; and *lay pastor,* with comprehensive ministry without a resident ordained pastor but under the supervision of a non-resident priest moderator.

All three are vital to the continued health and potential growth of parishes. It is the latter two, however, the pastoral associate and lay pastor, because of their comprehensive roles, which will need chapters further explaining the functions of each in greater detail.

Notes

1. It is important to note that Pope Paul VI's *Ministeria quaedam* (August 15, 1972) limits *institution* of the ministries of "acolyte" and "lector" to men. In the new code this is continued in canon 230, §1.

According to *Ministeria quaedam,* these are the requirements for admission to these ministries: petition signed by the aspirant to the ordinary; suitable age and special qualities determined by the episcopal conference; firm will to give faithful service to God and the Christian people; conferral by the ordinary.

The new code, canon 230, §§2 and 3, states that lay people can receive a temporary assignment to the role of lector in liturgical actions. Where needed, they can through their baptismal ministry exercise the ministry of the Word, preside over liturgical prayers, confer baptism, and distribute Holy Communion.

Most dioceses and parishes have not formally installed lectors and acolytes but have trained both women and men to function in these "temporary" roles. Unfortunately, due in part to many parishes using the official canonical terms of lector and acolyte there is much confusion and some scandal caused by this. Therefore, it is appropriate to use terms other than "lector" and "acolyte" unless one is officially installed by the ordinary. "Reader" and "Eucharistic minister" serve this purpose well.

2. On July 1, 1985, Sr. Eunice A. Hittner, O.S.F., was appointed lay pastor intern of St. Rose Catholic Church, Monroe, Oregon, as well as Our Lady of Victory, a mission parish in Harrisburg, Oregon. She is expected to receive official canonical appointment by Archbishop Cornelius Power.

2

An Introduction to Canon Law

Introduction

> *A journey, literally a generation long, has just drawn to a conclusion, as exactly twenty-four years have passed since the unforgettable Pope John XXIII announced a reform of the Code, together with the proclamation of the Council.*[1]

With these words Pope John Paul II made this declaration on February 3, 1983, in the Hall of Benedictions over the portico of St. Peter's Basilica on the occasion of the solemn presentation of the New Code of Canon Law. Presenting it to the assembled audience, he then added, "*Tolle, lege*" ("Take [it], read [it]"), giving permission to have the code translated into the vernacular, subject to the approval of the appropriate episcopal conferences, so that *all* of "Christ's faithful" would have direct access to it.

Two aspects of this promulgation of the new code (which took effect November 27, 1983), need further comment: permission to translate into the vernacular and the address to "Christ's faithful." Seemingly minor points for the uninitiated, they have tremendous explosive potential for how we understand and act on the new code.

The old Code of Canon Law of 1918 had only one official version, the Latin text itself. Granted, Latin was then still a living language for the Church in its liturgical rites and virtually everyone knew a few words or phrases. Yet a working knowledge of Latin was basically the province of clerics. Any "translation" of the old code was to be considered not an official translation but an "interpretation" or "commentary." Thus, access to the old code was effectively limited to clerics, who shared in the governing body of the hierarchy. The laity, the "governed," had little reason to be interested in Church law. Clerics would inform them as needed about any laws which applied to them.

By encouraging episcopal conferences to oversee and make available translations of this new code, Pope John Paul II has given "Christ's faithful" direct access to their own heritage and provides them with the tools they need to continue to become the People of God called forth by the spirit and documents of Vatican II.

The term "Christ's faithful" is an entirely new one in the code. It emanates from the spirit of Vatican II. First, the old code used the term "the faithful" when speaking of the laity as distinct from the clergy. This new term of "Christ's faithful" addresses the whole People of God together, called to the same witness and mission. Second, the emphasis is on fidelity to Christ, not to the Church itself as primary, with the new code then seen as that which enables us to do that within this particular ecclesial communion.

Each of us, then, as part of "Christ's faithful" is called to "take and read" this new code. It is the document which gives shape, form, and direction to the vision of Vatican II, a vision we are all called to share through baptism. It is the way we are able to embody the gospel ideals in fidelity to Christ and in communion with the Catholic Church.

Background of the Old Code

How did the Catholic Church develop a code of canon law

in the first place? The process, understandably, is not widely known. Over the centuries practically every general council made some laws which had some application to the universal Church. From time to time these collections would be assembled, the best known being the Code of Canon Law of 1918. It was not an attempt to recast the legal system or adapt it to the needs of the modern world but merely to systematize and collate a confusing collection of Church laws. The laity in the old code received scant attention, except in terms of their being subject to excommunication and other censures.

We now have a new code of canon law, but we must resist the temptation to see it merely as an updated version of the old model. It is so alluring to just substitute a new legalism for an old one, but if we try to do this to the new code we both violate its spirit and its prophetic call to witness. How we are going to understand this new code is much more important than even a detailed knowledge of the 1752 canons it contains.

How to Interpret the New Code

In seminaries, the teaching of the old code always fell under moral theology because it dealt with how we were to be saved. The decree issued by John Paul II on January 25, 1983, makes it very clear that this new code is not to be a law of salvation but a document meant for a community of believers. To do justice to the interpretation of the new code in this light we must keep several things in mind:[2]

1. This new code is now part of ecclesiology, the study of the Church, and is a part of who we are as a community of believers. It is not a document giving a blueprint on how to be saved.

2. On the one hand we must take seriously the importance of Church law. This community of people is a visible, organized witness to God's presence in the world. The law is a part of our ability to be an effective sign of that presence. On the other hand, we must remember two things. First, the law

is a skeleton, which gives shape and strength to the body, but always needs God's spirit to animate it. Second, the new code is already out of date and serves a conservative function as a kind of memory bank which remembers past practice and makes it available to us. *It is always behind the practice,* for pastoral practice is more than the law and leads the law.

3. We must see the new code as it was first intended by Pope John XXIII, as a renewal of the whole Church and an updating of Church law in light of the renewal. The council is to be the way we understand the code, not the other way around. This leads us to see that:

- The Church is a *community of persons,* not a hierarchically dominated state.
- This community is *fundamentally equal* through baptism. No longer is the Church to be seen as a two-tiered society.
- *Subsidiarity* is a basic working principle. This means that the responsibility of governing and decision-making is not to be found at the highest level, but at the most appropriate level. Bishops, dioceses, and parishes are to have more of an impact on participating in governing rather than just being governed from above.
- The official ministry of the Church is not to be one of status and privilege, but one of service.

How the New Code Attempts to Implement the Council

The structure of the new code is the key to understanding its nature. To see how radical it is, it is first necessary to look briefly at the structure of the old code.

The Code of Canon Law of 1918 was rooted in the fourfold structure of Roman law: (1) general norms (how to understand law), (2) persons, (3) things (included are sacraments, magisterium, Church property, indulgences, etc.), (4) actions (procedures in the Church, with an extensive closing section on ecclesial sanctions).

The new code is entirely different in its organization:

Book I: *General Norms*

Book II: *People of God*

- applies to all people
- the "rules of office" are here rather than in a special clergy section, showing clergy as part of the community and opening up offices to anyone, lay or cleric, with the proper qualifications

Books III, IV, and V answer this question: How do we understand the mission of Jesus? We do this by helping Jesus bring about the Kingdom of God by exercising our threefold *munera* ("gifts") as prophetic, priestly, and kingly people.

Book III: *The Teaching Office of the Church*

- the prophetic charism emphasizes that the ministry of teaching belongs to the Church as a whole

Book IV: *The Sanctifying Office of the Church*

- the priestly charism states that the call to sanctification is addressed equally to all the baptized

Book V: *The Kingly Office of the Church*

- the kingly/servant charism, deals with the governance of temporal goods

Book VI: *Sanctions in the Church*

- this section considerably reduced in the new code
- recognizes Church as community of disciples, not a civil government with a penal law

Book VII: *Processes*

- deals with trials and tribunals
- explains the rights of any person to plead before the appropriate Church court to seek justice

Summary

The new code can seem overwhelming to the neophyte. We can grasp its essential meaning, however, if we realize that it calls us to mission, to *munera* ("gifts"), and to ministry.

Call to mission. We are the People of God. Called through baptism, we are a community of equals. Through this baptismal call we are sent forth to share in the mission of Christ, to work for the salvation of human beings in and through earthly society. The Kingdom of God is not our identity as Church, but our purpose.

Call to munera *("gifts").* We can take part in this mission because we have a share in the threefold charism of Christ: we share in his prophetic, priestly, and kingly gifts. There is no longer to be an *ecclesia docens* ("teaching church") and an *ecclesia discens* ("listening church"), of clergy in the first, laity the second. We are *all* called to share actively in the gifts of Christ.

Call to ministry. Each of us is called to the five-fold ministry of the Church: evangelization, sanctification, works of mercy, renewal of the social order, and participation by some in the official pastoral ministry of the Church.

Notes

1. Keep in mind that this new code and the old code of 1918 are codes for the Latin Church, with other ritual Churches in union with the bishop of Rome having their own ecclesial laws.

2. The steps outlined here come from a talk given to the NOCERCC Convention, Feb. 7–11, 1983, by Fr. James Provost entitled "Justice in the Church."

3

Canon Law and the Rights and Responsibilities of the Baptized

The Six Precepts of the Church in the 1918 Code of Canon Law

One of the most attractive aspects of the 1918 code was that what little the laity knew about it they knew well. Virtually anyone over forty with a minimum of Catholic education could answer this question: *"What are the six precepts of the Church?"*

- To assist at Mass on Sundays and Holy Days of Obligation
- To fast and abstain on certain days designated by the Church
- To receive Communion during the Easter season
- To confess our sins once a year
- To contribute what is necessary for divine worship and Church support
- To observe the Church's regulations on marriage

On the positive side, these precepts were both very clear and achievable with a small amount of effort. If we were able to meet those expectations, we knew we were in good standing in the eyes of the Church and, therefore, with Christ himself. If we failed somewhere we knew exactly what to do in order to regain our status. What we were called by the Church to do was to perform certain external actions which were visible to and overseen by the whole Church community.

On the negative side, these rules were both minimal and legalistic. They were *minimal* in that they laid out the outermost perimeters of Church membership to show us exactly how far we could go before we went beyond the protection of the Church. To be a practicing Catholic, according to the old code, would take about sixty hours a year. They were *legalistic* in that they spoke only to the external actions of the members, rather than the spirit behind the laws. Being physically present and "assisting" at Mass were all that the old code called for, with no words or directives to the call to be a community of prayer.

The Spirit of the 1983 Code of Canon Law

The spirit of the new code of canon law is totally different from the 1918 code in two very fundamental ways. First, the Church still lists precepts for its members, but the spirit with which they were written and are to be lived out is much different. Second, both accompanying and, in fact, interwoven with this new list of precepts is the equally important "Bill of Rights" for every Catholic, thus linking inextricably the responsibilities we have with the rights we possess as members of the Church and of Christ.

We can get a feel for the precepts, or responsibilities, in the new code by reading them over slowly:

- Preserve communion with the Church (c. 209, §1)
- Fulfill the duties attached to membership in the universal and particular Church (c. 209, §2)
- Lead a holy life (c. 210)
- Promote the growth and holiness of the Church (c. 210)
- Obligation to evangelize the nations (c. 211)
- Obey the teachings and statutes of Church pastors (c. 212, §1)
- Duty to recommend and inform public opinion (c. 212, §3)

- Support the Church's needs in liturgy, charity, and ministry (c. 222, §1)
- Promote social justice (c. 222, §2)
- Aid the poor from one's own resources (c. 222, §2)

For those of us weaned on the old precepts, our first reaction on reading this list is quite possibly one of shock. Then two questions surface: *How do we do them?* and *How do we know when we have done them?*

There is no simple answer—and that is the whole point. We find the spirit of the new code peeking through this list of new laws. We can see, quite easily, that these ten precepts are no longer a spiritual formula for successful Catholic life with carefully measured input (Mass on Sundays, Eucharist once a year, etc.), to guarantee the desired outcome—maintaining good standing in the Church. Instead we have a call to holiness—in our own lives, in the life of the Church, even to transforming the injustices of the social structures of secular government.

So, *How do we do them?* We do them daily in faith and in community, allowing the Spirit of the Lord to transform us and sanctify us. *When will we be finished with them?* Not until we have finished our own part of the journey as members of the pilgrim Church.

Examining the Precepts of the New Code of Canon Law

It is much harder to grab hold of the new precepts and claim that we have a firm grasp of their meaning and implications. It is important, however, to examine them more closely. They can be divided into four basic categories: membership in the Church; relationship to the world; relationship to Church authority; and obligation to justice.

Membership in the Church

We still do have obligations involved in Church membership. We are called to preserve communion with the Church (c. 209, §1) and to fulfill the duties involved in that communion, both at the local and on a universal level (c. 209, §2). In fact, we still have the obligation to receive Communion once a year (c. 920, §§ 1 and 2) and to confess once a year if in a state of serious sin (c. 989). Yet these two canons are no longer seen as an explanation of how we keep membership. They are located under their respective sacraments in Book IV, "The Sanctifying Office of the Church," not in Book II, "The People of God." They are meant to be seen then in the larger context of our call to be a People of God, a call to holiness and transformation of the social order (c. 210).

It is no longer sufficient to just be concerned for our own salvation, but we have an *obligation* to promote the growth and holiness of the Church. How we are to do that is left up to the individual's conscience, but *that* we are to do it is a given.

Relationship to the World

We can no longer be concerned with only the life in our Church community, but are obligated to evangelize the nations (c. 211). We do not do this by selling all our possessions and going to a foreign country. We can no longer do this by just handing over the obligation to evangelize to certain "specialists" in the Church called missionaries. Each of us, in our own way, is commanded to preach the gospel message of hope and salvation—because that is what *baptism* calls us to do, not a special vocation sent to a few later in life. Each of us must preach the gospel in whatever life we lead in the world.

Relationship to Church Authority

We still have an obligation to obey the teachings and statutes of Church pastors (c. 212, §1). That certainly has a familiar ring to it (most pastors would be delighted if their parishioners took this one seriously). Yet we are no longer to be divided along the old lines of the "teaching Church" (*ecclesia docens*) and "listening Church" (*ecclesia discens*). In the same canon is the duty, in keeping with our knowledge, competence, and position, to manifest to the pastors our views on matters which concern the good of the Church. We must also make our views known to others of Christ's faithful, always respecting faith and morals and with due reverence to authority.

This canon does not spell out how these two—obligation to pastors and obligation to make our views known—are to be balanced. It does, however, effectively obliterate that distinction between the teaching Church and the listening Church. We are all called, each with our own charisms, to be part of both the teaching Church and listening Church. We are called to both teach one another and listen to one another, governed by the spirit of love and humility.

Obligation to Justice

In the old code our financial obligations to the Church usually meant contributing to the Sunday collection, with Church pastors designating the allocating of the money. The new code does not *remove* our financial commitments, but expands them.

Canon 222, §1 obliges "Christ's faithful" to provide for the needs of the Church—in divine worship, in apostolic and charitable work, in support of its ministers. This gets us right back to the threefold *munera* of Christ—as priest, king, prophet. We have an obligation flowing from our own priestly call through baptism to be actively involved in divine worship. Our kingly call is one of apostolic and charitable work in the world. Our prophetic call is to support the ministries of the Church.

§2 of this canon points out that it is not even enough to do acts of mercy, but that we are called to "promote social justice." This means that we are obligated to work for the reform of all social institutions, civil and ecclesial, so that they may better reflect gospel values and support the God-given dignity of the human person.

The "Bill of Rights" in the New Code

Of equal importance and not to be seen apart from the list

of responsibilities of Church membership is the corresponding "Bill of Rights":

- Right to evangelize the nations (c. 211)
- Right to petition (c. 212, §2)
- Right to recommend (c. 212, §3)
- Right to hear the Word of God and to receive the sacraments from Church pastors (c. 213)
- Right to worship according to one's own ritual Church (c. 214)
- Right to one's own spirituality (c. 214)
- Right to form and direct religious associations (c. 215)
- Right to assembly (c. 215)
- Right to promote and support the apostolate (c. 216)
- Right to Christian education (c. 217)
- Right to academic freedom in religious studies (c. 218)
- Right to a free choice of one's state in life (c. 219)
- Right to one's reputation (c. 220)
- Right to privacy (c. 220)
- Right to legal defense (c. 221, §1)
- Right to due process (c. 221, §2)
- Right to legality in sanctions (c. 221, §3)

A detailed analysis of these rights is not needed here. It is necessary to know that we have these rights conferred on us through baptism. They are not "privileges" which may be revoked by Church authority.

Through baptism, we have the right:

- to evangelize and promote the apostolate
- to petition, recommend, to inform public opinion, to assembly, to Christian education, to academic freedom, to choosing a state in life
- to the Word of God and the sacraments, to our own ritual Church, to our own spirituality, to both form and direct religious associations
- to our own reputation, to privacy, to legal defense, to due process, to legality in sanctions

The Bill of Rights and Responsibilities: Call to Mission, Munera, *Ministry*

As "Christ's faithful" we are called through him and in him to be Christ for the world and to share in and continue his actions. We are called to the *mission* of Christ to reveal the kingdom of God through our call to holiness and our call to evangelize the nations in his name. We are called to the threefold *munera* ("gifts") of Christ: to be a priestly, kingly, prophetic people. We are called to the living out of the *ministry* of Christ in the world.

It is helpful to see these canons of rights and responsibilities of the baptized divided under these three headings: mission, *munera,* and ministry.

Call to Mission

Rights

- Right to evangelize the nations (c. 211)
- Right to hear the Word of God and receive the sacraments (c. 213)
- Right to worship according to one's own ritual Church (c. 214)
- Right to one's own spirituality (c. 214)
- Right to form and direct religious associations (c. 215)

Responsibilities

- Preserve full communion with the Church (c. 209, §1)
- Fulfill duties attached to membership in universal and particular Church (c. 209, §2)
- Lead a holy life (c. 210)
- Promote the growth and holiness of the Church (c. 210)
- Obligation to evangelize the nations (c. 211)

Call to Munera *("gifts")*

- Right to petition (c. 212, §2)
- Right to recommend (c. 212, §3)
- Right to public opinion (c. 212, §3)
- Right to assembly (c. 215)

- Obey the teachings and statutes of Church pastors (c. 212, §1)
- Duty to recommend and to inform public opinion (c. 212, §3)

Call to Ministry

- Right to support the apostolate (c. 216)
- Right to a Christian education (c. 217)
- Right to academic freedom in religious studies (c. 218)
- Right to a free choice of one's state of life (c. 219)
- Support the Church's needs in the areas of liturgy, works of charity, and the ministry (c. 222, §1)
- Promote social justice (c. 222, §2)
- Aid the poor from one's own resources (c. 222)

In addition, all of the baptized have a right to one's reputation (c. 220), and to one's privacy (c. 200). In order to protect one's rights in the Church, each person has a right to a legal defense (c. 221, §1), to due process (c. 221, §2), and to legality in sanctions (c. 221, §3).

Summary

We can see our rights and responsibilities in the new code through our call to mission, our call to *munera* ("gifts"), and our call to ministry.

Call to mission. Our mission as Church is to work for the Kingdom of God. We are called to holiness through Christ and in the Spirit, and we are called to evangelize the nations in the name of Christ.

Call to munera. Because we receive this call to participate in the mission of Christ through baptism and because we receive the "gifts" we need for that task in baptism, we are each called to share in the priestly, prophetic, and kingly charisms of Christ. Thus it is both our sacred obligation and God-given right not only to obey Church pastors but to be informed and speak out in areas of Church life in which we are qualified. What God has given through baptism the Church cannot take away.

Call to ministry. We have both a right and an obligation to develop the charisms we received through baptism. Thus we have rights to participate in the apostolate, to get the education we need to be effective, to choose the state of life in which we wish to follow Christ. We have not just the right, but the obligation, to participate in and through the Church in her works of liturgy, charity, and ministry, and the obligation to work for justice in the world.

4

The Code of Canon Law and Official Ministries

Introduction: A Recap of "Ministry" and "Official Ministries"

The preceding chapter dealt with our call to ministry through baptism. We receive this call then through the gift of the Holy Spirit, whose continuing presence urges us to do the work of Christ.

"Official ministry," what canon lawyers would term "office," is a stable function for a spiritual purpose which has been set up either by divine law or Church law. One would place under divine law the offices of pope and bishop. All other official ministries are the various ways the Church has organized over the centuries to carry out these functions. In some fashion the Church has always designated or commissioned certain people in the Church for certain ministries.

The Two Classes of Non-Priest Ministers in the New Code

The code, although it never defines ministry or official ministry, does much in a practical way towards shaping official ministry. It opens up the potential for broad participation in official ministry for those who are, in some way or another, designated ministers on behalf of or in the name of the Church. In this category are two kinds of non-priest ministers: *deacons* and *laity with special functions.*

Permanent Diaconate

In the wake of Vatican II, the office of permanent diaconate was restored, although it is presently limited to men only, unlike the practice of the early Church. As the numbers of priests continued to decline, many dioceses tried to fill in the holes created by their exodus by building up the permanent diaconate. Often their desperation to fill vacancies and their zeal to recreate a renewed ministry led them rapidly forward, well ahead of any long-term pastoral planning, a well balanced and theologically sound understanding of permanent diaconate, or a thoughtful discussion of the possibilities of lay ministry.

TITLES AND RIGHTS

Even now, years after the permanent diaconate was reestablished, there is still much confusion about it, even among clergy. Not only laity speak of the "lay deacon." We must remember that, according to canon law, the diaconate is an ordained ministry. Even permanent deacons are ordained and are thus bound under the new code. If a canon in the new code uses the phrase, "cleric," it applies to *all* those in ordained ministry: bishops, priests, deacons. Thus, permanent deacons have the right to solidarity with other clerics, a right to spiritual support, a right to continuing education, etc.

FUNCTION OF THE DEACON

A deacon may preach, including the homily during Mass; may baptize and conduct funeral services; distribute the Eucharist and take it to the sick. In addition, he may preside at liturgical services, witness marriage, and provide exorcisms as part of the Rite of Christian Initiation for Adults (RCIA).

AREAS OF CONCERN

With the exception of the official homily at Mass and the need for the Episcopal Conference to secure permission from the Holy See for laity to officiate at marriages (c. 1112, § 1), laity can legitimately perform all of the diaconal functions listed above. We need both wisdom and pastoral experience to avoid conflicts between deacons and official lay ministers and confusion on the part of the parishioners (and clergy).

We need to beware of just setting up another hierarchical, clerical class between laity and priests. We must decide whether or not to continue an exclusively male ministry when laity of both sexes are performing virtually all of the functions of the diaconate as part of their role as official lay ministers. We must question the practice of using permanent deacons who might be functioning minimally in a parish while holding down a full-time job elsewhere supplanting a full-time official lay minister when a "sacramental" moment arrives. We must realize that many laity in professional Church ministry have equal and sometimes greater pastoral experience and theological education than a diaconal program might provide for its permanent deacons.

It is thus crucial, *first,* to work out a better theology of the permanent diaconate. *Second,* we must realize that laity in official ministry can do and are doing virtually everything that a permanent deacon can do. *Third,* we need to work out a better relationship between the deacon and professional lay minister. *Fourth,* we must continue to explore whether the diaconate is exclusivist and sexist.

Official Lay Ministry

The first response to the growing shortage of clergy, as mentioned above, was the almost immediate implementation of the permanent diaconate in the late 1960s. The "second generation" of people called forth by the needs of the Church is a rapidly growing number of men and women entering lay ministry—due in part to the problems raised in the section on permanent diaconate, in part to the workings of the Holy Spirit. It is largely in their hands that the future of the Church of the twenty-first century rests.

The tools which lay ministers bring to the work of building up the Church are many: their spirit, sense of adventure, ability to take risks, adaptability to a rapidly changing ecclesiology, and, perhaps most important, their sense of humor under pressure.

In the new code are a number of canons which spell out the ways professional lay ministers will be functioning in the Church in the very near future. These canons fall into five headings: pastoral role, baptism, Eucharist, marriage, preaching.

Canons Relating to the Delegation of Professional Lay Ministers to Sacramental and Liturgical Ministry[1]

General Mandate and Pastoral Role

There are three canons which frame the involvement of the laity in the pastoral role of the Church.

Canon 230, §3 states that, where the needs of the Church require and ministers are not available, lay people, even if not lectors or acolytes, may exercise the ministry of the Word, preside over liturgical prayers, confer baptism and distribute Communion, in accordance with the provisions of the law.

Canon 517 states that, where circumstances require, the pastoral care of a parish, or a number of parishes together, can be entrusted to several priests jointly, with one priest being designated as moderator of the pastoral care exercised. This moderator is the one to be responsible to the bishop. If there is a shortage of priests, a bishop may entrust a deacon or some other person who is not a priest to share in the exercise of pastoral care of a parish, with a priest moderator also appointed by the bishop to supervise and direct the pastoral care.

Canon 519 states that the parish priest is the proper pastor of the parish entrusted to him. He exercises the pastoral care of the parish under the authority of the bishop, whose ministry he shares. He is to carry out the offices of teaching, sanctifying, and governing with the cooperation of other priests or deacons and with the assistance of lay members of Christ's faithful, according to the law.

It is not necessary here to examine minutely the potential ramifications of these three canons. It is, however, important to discover what all three have in common. (1) Laity, through baptism, share in the pastoral responsibilities of teaching, sanctifying, and governing. (2) Where necessary, they may be delegated to perform certain liturgical and sacramental functions which were formerly reserved to priests.

Baptism

The major canon regarding baptism is canon 861.

Canon 861 states that the ordinary minister of baptism is a bishop, a priest, or a deacon. If the ordinary minister is absent *or impeded,* a catechist or some other person deputed by the local ordinary may lawfully confer baptism. In a case of necessity, any person with the proper intention may do so.

There are two important points in this canon. The first regards the interpretation of the phrase "absent or impeded." If the parish priest is not absent, in what way might he be impeded? Through illness? Another commitment in the parish? Or even, possibly, through the realization that the catechist who has been entrusted with the faith formation of the parents might be the more fitting minister of the sacrament for their child? Only pastoral practice will clarify this ambiguity.

The second point is that a lay person may be "lawfully" deputed to confer baptism by the local ordinary. There is still a provision that anyone may baptize in an emergency, but now permission may also be granted in a non-emergency situation for a lay person to be the official minister of the sacrament.

Eucharist

The two key canons are canon 911, §2 and canon 943.

Canon 911, §2 states that in case of necessity, and with at least the presumed permission of the parish priest, any priest or *other minister of Holy Communion* may bring the Eucharist to the sick.

Canon 943 states that the minister of exposition of the blessed Sacrament and of the Eucharistic blessing is a priest or deacon. In special circumstances the exposition, but not the blessing, may be performed by an acolyte, an extraordinary minister of Holy Communion or another person deputed by the local ordinary, in accordance with regulations of the bishop.

The main pastoral implication of these two canons is the realization that our right to the Eucharist, in case of necessity, is greater than our dependence on clergy to provide it. Properly designated lay people have both the right and the duty to make sure that the baptized have access to the Eucharist and may take Communion to those in need, and only *subsequently* have to inform the proper priest, for permission is to be presumed.

Marriage

The applicable canon is canon 1112.

Canon 1112 states that, where there are no priests or deacons, the diocesan bishop can delegate lay persons to witness marriages, if (1) the Episcopal Conference has given its prior approval; and (2) if permission of the Holy See has been obtained. A suitable lay person is to be selected who is capable of giving instruction to those getting married and fitted to conduct the marriage liturgy properly.

It is not that unusual for lay people to witness marriages. Even the old code of canon law had provision for this. Code 1098 states that if the parish priest or ordinary or priest delegate cannot be approached without serious inconvenience that in danger of death a marriage contract in front of witnesses is both valid and licit. Even outside the danger of death, this is allowed if it can be prudently foreseen that this situation will last for a month. The major difference, then, in the new code is that the situation does not have to be extraordinary in nature, but may become an ordinary way of providing witnesses for church marriages, assuming an Episcopal Conference gives its approval and solicits and obtains permission from the Holy See.

Preaching

The applicable canons are 759, 766, and 767, §1.

Canon 759 states that lay members of Christ's faithful, by reason of their baptism and confirmation, are witnesses to the good news of the Gospel, by their words, and by the example of their Christian lives. They can be called to cooperate with bishops and priests in the exercise of the ministry of the Word.

Canon 766 states that the laity may be allowed to preach in a church or oratory in certain circumstances where necessary or where, in particular cases, it would be advantageous, according to the provisions of the Episcopal Conference and without prejudice to canon 767, §1.

Canon 767, §1 states that the most important form of preaching is the homily, which is part of the liturgy, and is reserved to a priest or deacon. In the course of the liturgical year, the mysteries of faith and the rules of Christian living are to be expounded in the homily from the sacred text.

Through our baptism we, as Christ's faithful, are witnesses to the Gospel and can be called upon to exercise the ministry of the Word. There are circumstances where it would not only be necessary but even advantageous for a lay person to be the preacher in a church or oratory, although these circumstances are not spelled out. Although only a deacon or priest may give a homily at the Eucharist, this canon does not preclude, necessarily, a qualified lay person preaching in addition to or instead of a homily. Again, pastoral practice will be the testing ground of this canon.

Summary

It is very clear that in the new code laity are called to share much more fully in the pastoral role of the Church. In baptism, Eucharist, marriage, and preaching there are new avenues opening up for "official ministries." Exactly how and in what ways and when this will happen is not spelled out—and should not be—in the new code. It is through a prayerful examination of pastoral practices as they develop that we will learn what gifts these canons may bring to flower in the Church of the twenty-first century.

Notes

1. Canon Law Society of America, *Code of Canon Law: Latin–English Edition* (Washington: Canon Law Society of America, 1983).

5

The Pastoral Associate

Introduction

Most parishes in the near future, and many parishes now, have professional lay ministers who share with the pastor in the overall pastoral care of the parish. They serve in a comprehensive fashion—in liturgy, catechesis, pastoral care, and administration. The titles are not yet carved in stone, but they do need to somehow describe the function they serve.

The Title of "Pastoral Associate"

There is an old Hasidic tale which claims that as soon as people build an altar to God, his fire will most assuredly fall elsewhere. That may be what will happen to the emerging title of "pastoral associate" as a designation for a lay person(s) on a parish staff with comprehensive ministry in a parish. This term has value for two major reasons: (1) it points out that this person shares in the pastoring role of the pastor; (2) it indicates that this person is part of a ministry with shared responsibility to the parish.

There are two potential pitfalls for this new title—one involving underuse, the other overuse. On the one hand, there are people in many parishes now who are already functioning as pastoral associates, either through their official job description or more likely a gradual evolution of their job due to pastoral needs. They may still, however, be called other names, such as catechist, parish minister, director of religious education. On the other hand, there is a tendency in some parishes to attach this title to anyone with any kind of pastoral ministry in the parish, including youth minister, minister to the sick, C.C.D. coordinator, etc. Both are equally harmful.

The title "pastoral associate" should be used both sparingly and correctly. While not to be seen as a position of honor within the body of the laity, ranking below pastor but above any other lay ministry, it must convey the function it serves. The one(s) with this title in a parish should be on the staff, usually full time, with officially designated responsibilities to the whole parish with involvement in *all* areas of pastoral life in the parish: liturgy, catechetics, pastoral care, and administration. Other ministers with a specific area of ministry, such as music or youth ministry, are not to be called "pastoral associates," but "parish ministers" or some other title specifying their role.

And so, what kind of a person becomes a pastoral associate? What are their professional qualifications? To whom are they accountable? What are some possible areas of ministry?

Professional Qualifications[1]

Personal

Candidates should be mature, responsible, possess integrity, initiative, flexibility, and prayerfulness.

Experiential

These people come to their position from work and life experience which have given evidence of the exercise of baptismal commitment. In living out this commitment, the candidate should have manifested fidelity to the Catholic Church, leadership ability, facility in interpersonal relations, and interest in community service.

Academic

The ideal academic education is a master's degree, or its equivalent in theology, pastoral ministry, or religious education. The degree program should include fundamental theology, sacramental theology, moral theology, social justice, Scripture, ecclesiology, liturgy, and pastoral counseling. In addition there should be practicums in pastoral ministry.

Accountability

Pastoral associates are hired by and accountable to the person(s) having pastoral care of a parish, usually an ordained pastor. They should work under contract which may initially be for one year, then renewable for multiple years. The contract should include provisions for evaluation, conciliation, and arbitration procedures. In developing these on a parochial level, each parish must keep in mind both the new code of canon law and any applicable diocesan documents or procedures on conciliation or arbitration.

Possible Areas of Ministry

The pastoral associate is to be involved in all areas of parish ministry: in overall administrative functions; in liturgy; in catechesis; in pastoral care. The following list, in each of these four areas, is to be used as a guideline only. On the one hand, there may well be particular items a parish may wish to include. On the other, we must bear in mind that no *one* person could possibly ever perform *all* these functions.

General Area of Ministry

The pastoral associate may participate in the parish pastoral council, the parish staff, the area vicariate, the archdiocesan pastoral synod, and various committees and commissions. In addition, he/she may be involved in ecumenical and ministerial associations and dialogues.

Ministry of Liturgy

Here there are many possibilities:

- Being involved in the liturgy-worship commission in a parish
- Sharing in planning/evaluation of Sunday homilies and other special liturgies (seasonal, children's, etc.)
- Recruiting/training/scheduling eucharistic ministers
- Preaching (subject to canon law and norms of local Church)
- Sharing in planning of communal penance services
- Participating in planning and coordination of RCIA during Mass
- Working with couples planning marriage
- Witnessing weddings, if authorized by the bishop
- Providing guidance and direction to families arranging funerals
- Presiding at wake services and graveside services, when needed
- Sharing in the planning and coordination of the RCIA
- Presiding at daily Communion services and on Sunday Communion services, subject to regulations of the code and norms of local Church
- Being an official minister of baptism, where needed and authorized

Ministry of the Word

Here, too, are many possible areas of ministry:

- Participating in the Religious Education Commission of a parish
- Coordinating and directing sacramental catechesis
- Sharing in developing/implementing an evangelization program
- Directing and assisting in all stages of the catechumenate

- Organizing and facilitating Bible studies, prayer groups, Lent/Advent discussion; Sunday reflections on the readings of the day
- Directing and/or teaching adult education programs
- Being a resource person for religious education programs

Ministry of Pastoral Services

Here, again, are many possibilities:

- Participating in mission/social concerns/social action commissions
- Coordinating pastoral care of the sick and elderly and training parishioners to get involved in this care
- Providing emergency Communion for the sick
- Acting as advocate for the needs of parishioners (monetary, medical, social); making referrals when necessary
- Organizing parish programs to respond to local needs
- Organizing jail ministry, being involved in community corrections
- Being a liaison for parish and community to meet needs of poor
- Facilitating parish awareness and response to peace and justice issues
- Working on marriage cases and training notaries
- Providing counseling and support to individuals and families
- Developing and facilitating community-building activities
- Sharing in planning and directing of retreats, days of reflection
- Serving as spiritual advisor for parish committees and groups

Summary

It should be obvious that any person who can perform the functions listed above must be highly qualified and trained, for this position entails serious responsibility towards the parish. We perform no service by placing an unqualified person in this demanding job with vague hopes that this person *may* work out or pick up the needed skills in time.

Some dioceses are moving in the direction of certification of pastoral associates, required for anyone serving in this capacity. That may or may not come about, but we must be aware that a pastoral associate has serious responsibility and is also entitled to just wage, contract, stipulation of rights, grievance procedures, and due process.

Notes

1. The sections on Professional Qualifications, Accountability, and Possible Areas of Ministry are taken from a working document prepared jointly by the Pastoral Associates of Oregon and the Vicariate of Worship and Ministries in the archdiocese of Portland, Oregon, in 1984.

6

The Lay Pastor

Introduction

The position of the lay pastor has one major advantage over "pastoral associate." Whereas the latter is a combination of a title emerging from pastoral experience and functions which are culled from various canons relating to "official ministry," the former, "lay pastor," does find an easily located home in the new code of canon law. Canon 517, which creates the position of lay pastor (also called "pastoral facilitator" or "pastoral administrator"), is important enough to quote in full:

> When circumstances require it, the pastoral care of a parish or of several parishes together can be entrusted to a team of several priests *in solidum* with the requirement, however, that one of them should be the moderator in exercising pastoral care, that is, he should direct their combined activity and answer for it to the bishop.
>
> If the diocesan bishop should decide that due to a dearth of priests a participation in the exercise of the pastoral care of a parish is to be entrusted to a deacon or to some other person who is not a priest or to a community of persons, he is to appoint some priest endowed with the powers and faculties of a pastor to supervise the pastoral care.[1]

It was necessary under the 1918 code that a priest canonically appointed by the ordinary reside within the territory of a parish. If he resided elsewhere but was the sacramental and liturgical overseer of a nearby church, it was designated not as a parish but as a mission.

The new code creates two new positions: that of a lay person who can be responsible for sharing in the pastoral care of a parish, through canonical appointment by the bishop, and that of a priest who, while not resident in the parish, has supervisory functions over the lay person in residence. The code, however, does not give these persons specific titles. The term "priest moderator" will be used to designate the priest responsible for the supervision of another parish and the term "lay pastor" will be used for the person canonically appointed by the bishop to be responsible for the exercise of pastoral care in a parish with no resident priest. These two working together are responsible for the pastoral care of a parish and together replace the parish priest appointed as pastor.

There is no separate section in canon law which spells out the respective duties of a lay pastor and priest moderator. Therefore, it is necessary to examine the canons enumerating the responsibilities of a parish priest to see in what ways a lay pastor and priest moderator working together are to fill them. There are four major areas of responsibility for a parish priest (and by implication a lay pastor and priest moderator): liturgical, teaching, pastoral care, and administrative. These areas reflect back on the threefold *munera* of Christ and, therefore of all the baptized faithful, to be priest, prophet, and king. Liturgical responsibilities flow from the priestly call, teaching from the prophetic, pastoral care and administration from the call to kingly service.

Liturgical Responsibilities[2]

The general principal of liturgical responsibility on the part of the parish priest is contained in canon 528, §2. The parish priest must make the Eucharist the center of the parish assembly; nourish the faithful through celebrating the sacraments, especially the Eucharist; bring the faithful to family prayer as well as a knowing and active participation in the sacred liturgy; supervise liturgy in his parish, being vigilant lest any abuses creep in. They must also make sure that those who seek the sacraments are properly prepared and evangelized.

Baptism

The parish priest is entrusted with the administration of baptism (c. 530, §1). He is also responsible for proper catechesis of the parents (c. 851, §2); instructing the faithful in the correct manner of baptizing in danger of death (c. 861, §2); seeing that a name foreign to Christian mentality is not given the child (c. 855); ascertaining eligibility of sponsors and providing them when needed (c. 874); keeping the sacred oils (c. 847, §2); keeping the records (cc. 535, 877).

For infants, the lay pastor (cc. 230, 861) can be deputed by the bishop to baptize under supervision of the priest moderator. The lay pastor could also be given the obligation of preparation and be delegated by the priest moderator to record the baptism. For adults, the issue is more complex. Canon 866 states that the adult who is baptized is to be confirmed immediately unless a grave reason prevents it. The ordinary minister of confirmation is a bishop, although a priest can validly confer it if he has the faculty to do so, either from general law or by way of a special grant from the competent authority (c. 882). General law allows a parish priest to confirm when he baptizes an adult or admits a baptized adult into full communion with the Catholic Church. Any priest may confirm in danger of death.

There is an interesting lacuna in the law here. When baptism and confirmation are performed at the same time, the one who actually baptizes also confirms (c. 883, §2). Strictly speaking, then, the priest-presider at the Eucharistic liturgy where these two sacraments take place would have to do both, baptize and confirm. In past Church history, however, deacons and deaconesses would baptize, then lead the neophytes to the bishop for confirmation. A broad interpretation of canon law might suggest the possibility of lay pastors or catechists baptizing, doing so under the supervision of the priest moderator, who is presiding over the baptism of the catechumens, although not pouring the water.

Confirmation

As stated above, the ordinary minister of confirmation is a bishop. A parish priest may confirm an adult just baptized or one coming into full communion with the Catholic Church. Any priest has the faculty to confirm in danger of death. In addition, the parish priest is responsible for instructing the faithful regarding this sacrament, keeping the sacred oils and accurate parish records.

The lay pastor can be considered responsible for sacramental catechesis. In addition, the priest moderator may assign the lay pastor responsibility for recording the confirmation in the parish books.

Eucharist

The celebration of the Eucharist on Sunday and holy days of obligation falls to the parish priest (c. 530, §7). He is also to instruct the faithful on the doctrine of the Eucharist and to supervise the catechesis of children preparing for it. He is entrusted with administering Viaticum to the sick.

When necessity warrants, lay persons may preside over liturgical prayers and distribute Communion (c. 230). Where there is no priest to celebrate the Eucharist, a lay person may preside at a Liturgy of the Word and distribute Communion on Sundays or holy days of obligation. Any person who is a minister of Communion may take Viaticum to the sick in case of necessity. Where there is no parish priest, the lay pastor is to preside over Sunday Communion services and distribute Communion to the sick. Viaticum, Eucharistic catechesis, and First Communions are conducted by the lay pastor under the supervision of the priest moderator.

Penance

The parish priest and those who take his place possess the faculty to hear confession within their jurisdiction (c. 968, §1). The faithful should have easy access to this sacrament, on days and hours set for their convenience (c. 986, §1).

The lay pastor may instruct the faithful about the sacrament of reconciliation and may conduct communal reconciliation services without individual confession or absolution. The lay pastor should work closely with the priest moderator to make sure that the needs of the faithful are being met in regards to regular access to sacramental confession.

Anointing of the Sick

The administration of this sacrament, along with the imparting of the apostolic blessing, is entrusted to the parish priest (c. 530, §3). Pastors are to see that the sick are supported by this sacrament at the appropriate time (c. 1001). The parish priest is to obtain the sacred oils from the bishop and keep them in a fitting manner. Any priest in case of necessity can bless the oil used in this sacrament, but only in the celebration of this sacrament (c. 999, §2).

The lay pastor cannot sacramentally anoint but shares in the pastoral care of the sick in the parish. The lay pastor must work closely with the priest moderator to make sure he can be called in for Viaticum, anointings, and confirmation in danger of death.

Funerals

The performing of funerals is a function especially entrusted to the parish priest (c. 530, §5). The lay pastor may conduct a memorial service of the Word, including the distribution of Communion, and may also conduct the cemetery service.

Marriage

There are many canons regarding the sacrament of marriage, regarding eligibility, impediments, pastoral preparation, the ceremony, recording, etc. Obviously, the priest moderator would need to be aware of them. At the moment, witnessing marriages is limited to priests and deacons.

The lay pastor may be responsible for much, if not all, of the catechetical instruction of the couple and needs to be aware of all of the canons relating to this sacrament. Canon 1112 allows the diocesan bishop to delegate lay persons to be official witnesses if the Episcopal Conference votes affirmatively and if permission of the Holy See is obtained. In any case, it is vital that both the responsibilities and the rights of a lay pastor regarding this sacrament be spelled out clearly in a way that is both faithful to the Code and sensitive to pastoral needs.

Summary Statement on Liturgical Responsibilities

There is no guarantee yet that those to be lay pastors have received appropriate liturgical and canonical education regarding their responsibilities and their relationship to the priest moderator. In the future it will be easier as norms and appointment and certification procedures are worked out, but for now it is important that each diocese develop guidelines which include both the responsibilities of the lay pastor and also appropriate liturgical texts for his or her use in areas of baptism, funerals, Sunday liturgies of the Word and, eventually, marriage.

Teaching Responsibilities

The fundamental canon describing the teaching responsibility of the parish priest is canon 528, §1. The parish priest must see that: the Word of God in its entirety is announced to the faithful; that the lay Christian faithful are instructed in the faith, especially in the homilies and through catechetical formation he is to give. He is to foster works which promote the Gospel, including issues involving social justice; to be concerned with education of children and young adults; to bring the gospel message to those who have stopped practicing their religion.

With the exception of the homily in the strict sense, all of these obligations can be assigned to the lay pastor supervised by a priest moderator.

Preaching

The homily is reserved to a priest or deacon. In it, the mysteries of faith and the norms of Christian living are to be expounded from the sacred text throughout the liturgical year. When a congregation is present, a homily is to be given on Sundays and holy days of obligation, and is not to be omitted without serious reason. It is strongly recommended that a homily also be given at daily Mass, especially during Advent and Lent.

Lay persons may preach if it is necessary or useful in certain circumstances (c. 766). The lay pastor would obviously preach at the Sunday Liturgy of the Word when the priest moderator is absent. On those occasions when the priest moderator is present, it would seem that he is obliged to preach the homily (as distinguished from the lay pastor's sermon). Some canonists would allow a lay sermon without serious reason.

Catechetics

Pastors have a serious obligation to catechize the faithful so that their faith may become living and productive through formation in doctrine and experience of Christian living (c. 773). To accomplish this, the pastor is to employ the services of the faithful who are competent to assist in this enormous task (c. 776).

In accordance with norms established by the diocesan bishop the parish priest is to provide the following: catechesis for the celebration of the sacraments; further catechesis for children after their first Eucharist; catechesis for the handicapped, young people, and adults.

All of the provisions outlined above may be assigned to the lay pastor, under supervision of the priest moderator.

Summary Statement on Teaching Responsibilities

Teaching responsibilities can more easily be assigned to the lay pastor. It is essential, however, that these be spelled out in detail, particularly in regard to the lay pastor's relationship in this area to the priest moderator.

There is a rather intriguing lacuna in canon law regarding the assumption of these teaching responsibilities. Canon 833 requires that those who communicate the faith in some official capacity make a profession of faith in front of the proper ecclesiastical authority. This list includes those involved in Ecumenical Councils, particular councils, the synod of bishops or a diocesan synod, cardinals, bishops, diocesan administrators, all vicars, parish priests, rectors, professors of theology or philosophy at seminaries, deacons, rectors of ecclesiastical or Catholic universities, superiors in religious institutes and clerical societies of apostolic life.

There is no mention of either a priest moderator, who is not technically a parish priest, or of a lay pastor. Obviously both need to be faithful to doctrine and Church tradition, but it is an omission in the code to not have them make a profession of faith to the proper authorities.

Pastoral Responsibilities

Canon 529 lists the main areas of pastoral care and leadership development falling to the pastor of a parish. As a shepherd, the pastor is to provide visitation; minister to the sick; minister to those in special need, such as the poor, oppressed, lonely, migrants, and others in special need; and minister to family life. As a leader, the pastor is to involve the congregation in the Church's mission, especially through corporate action. He is also to promote a sense of membership in parish, diocesan, and universal community.

The lay pastor is called to the same responsibilities, always in cooperation with the priest moderator.

Administrative Responsibilities

The parish priest represents the parish in all juridic affairs, including parish property and income. Their duties as administrators are found in canons 1282 and 1289. Parish priests are limited to ordinary administrative acts.

When a lay pastor is appointed administrator of the parish by the bishop or administers the parish by delegation of the priest moderator, the lay pastor must be trained in these responsibilities, as detailed in the norms of canon law.

The business office of the diocese has a serious responsibility to make sure that there are definite guidelines regarding the administration of Church property according to canon law and that both the priest moderator and lay pastor understand them and accept the responsibility for fulfilling them.

Summary

It is highly probable that the position of lay pastor will have enormous impact in virtually every diocese in the United States within the next ten to twenty years. Thus it is essential that we understand it theologically and implement it properly, with due regard to parochial sensitivity and the norms of canon law.

Notes

1. Canon Law Society of America, *Code of Canon Law: Latin–English Edition* (Washington: Canon Law Society of America, 1983) 197.

2. This summary (excepting the section on pastoral care) is based on a paper prepared for the archdiocese of Portland, Oregon, by Fr. Bertram Griffin, entitled "The Parish Priest Moderator and the Lay Pastor."

7

Qualifications and Appointment of a Lay Pastor

Introduction

The role of a lay pastor is both demanding and comprehensive. There is not now any place where one can go to gain the theological competence and pastoral experience needed to specifically train for this position. It is a role which is just emerging. Dioceses which have pastoral associates (with or without that specific title) functioning in parishes will have a resource pool from which to draw as they set up guidelines for implementation of lay pastorates. Those dioceses that do not yet have laity involved in comprehensive ministry will have a harder time in preparing both laity and clerics to accept this new role and in finding qualified people to fill it.

Experience and Academic Background[1]

Neither academic training alone nor a background in various ministries without the educational experience equip one for the task of being a lay pastor. A combination of academic qualifications, past experience in ministry, personal talents and gifts, plus a desire for continuing professional growth need to be taken into account in the selection process.

Ideally, a lay pastor would have at least four years of working in the role of a pastoral associate, with responsibility in multiple areas of a parish: liturgy, pastoral care, administration, and teaching. If there is already a certification process for the position of pastoral associate, the one applying for a lay pastorate should already possess this certification. The candidate should ideally have a master's degree or its equivalent in theology, pastoral ministry or religious education, plus competency in areas of counselling, liturgical presidency, etc.

Other qualifications would include a scriptural and homiletic background for preaching; an ability to build a sense of community; background in marriage preparation, counseling, family life, and crisis management; familiarity with the RCIA; a knowledge of the code of canon law; ability to supervise budget management and office administration; experience working with pastoral councils; willingness to participate in diocesan and vicariate events; ability to work on a team with the sacramental minister, priest moderator, and offices of worship and ministry staff to develop this ministry; good physical health, as well as strong spiritual and psychological health.

Appointment and Conditions of Employment

Appointment

A person is to be hired by a local community which intends that this person is to be ultimately called canonically by the bishop as lay pastor of the parish. The length of time that person serves before canonical appointment will vary from parish to parish, the call normally coming through the parish's pastoral council.

Applicants need to be screened carefully by an interview committee from the parish. Since the appointment will ultimately be a canonical one, others involved in this process should include the priest moderator, the sacramental minister (if different from the priest moderator), the Vicar for Worship and Ministries (if the diocese has this office), and the professional counselor of the diocese who assists in the screening process of candidates for ordination. Final decision-making is the bishop's, since this is a canonical appointment. If the applicant is a religious, letters of recommendation are needed from both the community's director of personnel or ministry as well as the approval of the superior.

The résumé should include complete, updated transcripts of all academic work; letters of recommendation from both clerics and laity, indicating competence and experience in ministry; detailed description of pastoral experience, including proof of competency in liturgical leadership, teaching, preaching, counseling, pastoral care, and administrative experience. Appropriate certification in specific areas of ministry is needed in dioceses which have a certification process.

Conditions of Employment

1. SALARY AND BENEFITS

Salary should be commensurate with both the skills and the family situation of the candidate. Lay people in special service of the Church have a right to a just wage befitting their condition, whereby they can provide for their own needs and that of their families. Their benefits should include health insurance, social security, car, housing, and retirement plan, in line with diocesan policy for clerics. Vacation and study leave and retreat time should also be equal to that of clerics.

2. RESIDENCE

The lay pastor should live in the parish boundaries. If the parish facilities are unsuitable, more appropriate living accommodations need to be found and supplied by the parish, in accordance with the living standards of the parish.

3. TENURE

After a predetermined time as an intern, the canonically appointed lay pastor receives the same tenure as a diocesan priest.

4. TERMINATION

Canonically, only the bishop may terminate a lay pastor. In cases of dispute, referral should be made to the due-process board of the diocese.

5. CONTRACT AND EVALUATION

There need to be previously agreed upon times and methods for review of the contract and evaluation of the job performance of the lay pastor.

Certification of the Lay Pastor

As this ministry develops in a diocese as a major response to pastoral need, in all likelihood it may be advisable, even necessary, to move in the direction, on a diocesan level, of establishing and implementing a certification process to make sure the persons filling this role are competent in all areas of ministry.

Each diocese would then begin by setting up an official ministry certification board comprised of persons with both pastoral and theological background, both clerics and laity. The members should include those with background in canon law, Scripture, theology, liturgy, and pastoral ministry, since the lay pastor needs experience in each.

A skills/competency evaluation needs to be developed in each of the five areas listed above to assist the potential lay pastor in evaluating his or her own background and in completing any competencies lacking. The person(s) in each area of ministry on the certification board would be responsible for working with the candidate to make sure this competency was completed. The director of ministry in the diocese would oversee this process.

If a diocese goes in this direction, it is feasible, even desirable, to have a limited certification which has to be renewed periodically, based on satisfactory performance and ongoing education. The ministry certification board would be responsible for setting guidelines and reviewing certification of lay pastors.

Placement

Once someone is certified as a lay pastor, the diocese needs to decide how to be involved in that person's placement. It could be that the priest personnel board responsible for the placement of clergy could expand its task to include the placement of qualified, certified lay pastors as part of its responsibility to provide ministerial care of diocesan parishes. Or, the lay pastor may have to search out his or her own job possibilities and only later receive the canonical appointment of the bishop.

Notes

1. Taken from a 1984 document prepared by the office of ministries of the archdiocese of Portland, Oregon, titled "Proposed Guidelines Leading to Diocesan Policy for Pastoral Administrators."

8

Towards a Theology of Ministry: Current Issues

Introduction

It has been twenty years since the end of Vatican II, an event which has become "history" for a new generation of Catholics, too young to have much experiential knowledge of the explosive changes begun in the Church through its new vision, its documents, and its imperatives calling for change and growth. The most profound change may well be how we see ourselves as Church. No longer clergy/lay, "teaching"/"taught," those who have "vocations" and those who don't, the rest of us, we are together called, through our baptism, to share in the priestly, prophetic, and kingly ministry of Jesus Christ.

Yet old habits, old feelings, and old understandings of "Church" die hard. There are still many people in the Church who carry memories and attitudes that cannot simply be switched off as theology takes a different track. On the one hand, we need to be pastorally sensitive to those who have found these changes difficult and incomprehensible. On the other, we simply cannot quell the new workings of the Spirit in order to try to recapture the certitudes and safety we felt in the Church of the 1950s. Such differences in orientation still need to be resolved in the Church as we grow to a new awareness of ourselves as the People of God.

Columnist Frank Sheedy has addressed the question of what to do when there is no priest available for Sunday Mass.[1] (1) Is a Communion service a valid way to satisfy one's Sunday obligation? (2) Would it be holier driving to a town thirty miles away to attend Mass? Seemingly a simple question, both the question itself *and* Father Sheedy's response show an ecclesiology which is based neither on an understanding of the ecclesiology of Vatican II nor of the code of canon law. The columnist answers that one does not satisfy a Sunday obligation solely by receiving Communion. He then says that he himself does not find a thirty or forty minute drive unreasonable to fulfill the obligation. Finally, the writer does state that when Mass cannot be offered or attended, a Eucharistic prayer service is the next best thing.

If one wanted to find out the "letter" of the law, one would turn to canon 1248, where the obligation of assisting at Mass is reiterated. The code then continues on to say that because of the lack of a sacred minister or for other grave cause this is impossible, participation in a liturgy of the Word is recommended.

One must dig deeper than that to find the "spirit" in back of this legalistic answer to a legalistic question. What, for these two, constitutes a "grave reason"? The theology motivating both of them is one which sees "Eucharist" inextricably bound up with ordination to the priesthood and with absolutely no awareness of the value of the local place of worship or of the needs and gifts of the community gathered there. Attendance at a Mass offered by a priest thirty miles away is seen as "holier" and more virtuous, plus being a better fulfillment of the "obligation" than staying in one's own community to share the faith with one's own parish "family."

Recall that by the year 2000, in a survey cited in the introduction, there will be 54 percent fewer priests and 35 percent more Catholics than at the close of Vatican II. If these figures are accurate, the scenario pictured above would be common—a parish without a priest, or even a weekend helper, to be there on Sundays for Eucharistic worship.

We have two ways we can respond (simply refusing to recognize the rapid drop in numbers of clergy is not a choice but an act of cowardice). We can keep putting band-aids on our pre-Vatican II theology and think in terms of modern transportation providing all but those in the most rural, unevangelized, or rugged terrain with an easy "automobile" fix on Sundays. Or, we can really examine this approach to see the negative values it holds up for us in the name of "holiness."

As Catholic Christians, it is true that through baptism we join the universal Church and are truly members of any and all particular Catholic Churches by virtue of that sacrament. Yet we also have an equal right and obligation to live out that faith in the setting of the local Church. It is there that we break bread and worship together. It is there that we are welcomed into the universal Church through baptism, where we are received into Eucharistic communion, where we are married, where we are buried. It is with the other People of God in a particular community that we are called to live out our lives in faith.

If we understand this kind of Eucharistic faith, it becomes absurd at best and divisive at worst to see "virtue" in driving to a distant church on a Sunday when there is no priest to celebrate Mass at the parish church.

We are called through baptism to be a priestly, prophetic, and kingly people in service to one another and the world. What better way to show that and to live that then for the local congregation to assemble every Sunday to hear the Word of God and break bread together in a mutual sharing of faith? Wasn't that perceived need how the "obligation" to Sunday Mass came about in the first place—a need for the People of God to be a people celebrating and sharing together?

Do we really think it advisable to move in the direction of having fewer and fewer priests ministering to more and more people, where the sacraments will be less personal, less available? Or can we see this as an opportunity to (1) draw on the ministerial gifts of the local parishes; (2) question how ordained ministry can relate and *should* relate to the whole Church? Are our restrictions as to celibacy and gender essential to ordained ministry or do they perhaps stand in the way of a fuller and deeper understanding of ministry?

A Working Ecclesiology

Fr. James Provost (in his talk cited earlier) states that the most fundamental right of the People of God (and, interestingly, the only right for laity named in the 1918 code) is the "right to hear the word of God and to receive the sacraments." This is the fundamental right for all ministry because ministry is ultimately the proclaiming of the Gospel and the celebrating of the sacraments.

All the rest of the Church—its finances, procedures, sanctions, and general norms—must come from and go back to that central right and sacred obligation—to proclaim the Word and to participate in the sacraments. It is for the Church to decide how this is best to happen, to decide who is to minister, and what those restrictions for ministry are to be. What should yield first when the diminishing numbers of clergy make the Word of God and the sacraments more and more inaccessible?

In the pre-Vatican II Church ordained ministry had become separated from and independent from the community that should have given it meaning and shape. Absolute ordination, personal prerogatives, and indelible character of priesthood were terms which reflected an ecclesiology which saw ordained ministry as something personal, ontological, and removed from its function within the Church community.

Richard McBrien, in his book *Church: The Continuing Quest,* redefines "Church" in light of Vatican II, where the ministries *within* the Church are again connected to ministries *of* the Church:

> The church is the community of those who confess the Lordship of Jesus Christ, who ratify that faith in baptism, and who thereby commit themselves to membership and mission within that sacramental community of faith. But the primary reality is the Kingdom of God, and the existence and function of the Church make no sense apart from it. That mission is threefold in relationship to the reign of God: To proclaim in word and Sacrament the definitive arrival of the Kingdom in Jesus of Nazareth (kerygma), to offer itself as a test case of its own proclamation, as a group of people transformed by the Spirit into a community of faith, hope, love, and truthfulness—a sign of the Kingdom on earth and an anticipation of the Kingdom of the future (koinonia), and finally to realize and extend the reign of God through service in the socio-political order (diakonia).[2]

This definition highlights the relationship between the Christian community and the Kingdom preached by Jesus (note: the Church is not the kingdom, but somehow functions within and for it). While emphasizing the threefold mission of the Church to preach, to be a community of witness and sign, and to serve the world, this definition does not exclude the images alluded to in the documents of Vatican II: *communio,* sacrament, People of God, Body of Christ, seed, sheepfold, spouse of the Lamb.

Dimensions and Characteristics of Ministries of the Future

In keeping with this more biblical understanding of the Church and her ministry, and in light of both the Vatican documents and developing ministries in pastoral practice, ministry itself will be changing in many new ways in the near future. In an address presented to the annual general meeting of the Canadian Law Society in Ottawa in 1974, Fr. James Coriden predicted what some of the major changes would be:

1. Profusion of ministries, both baptized and official

2. Adaptability and flexibility of ministry as Church needs change
3. Specialization in some areas of ministry (counseling, liturgical celebration, social action, marriage work)
4. Ideal of professionalism growing
5. De-clericalization of ministry, both in expansion of ministries and in relationship of clerics to laity
6. Expanding roles of women in virtually all areas of ministry
7. Mobility of ministers increasing, due to general mobility of society and needs of special ministries
8. Some ministers may provide part or all of their own financial support.
9. Regular salary for both clerical and lay full-time professionals to replace clerical supplements such as stipends, stole fees, etc.
10. Rate of vocational change will continue to be high.
11. Greater responsibilities and positions of leadership entrusted to clerical and lay ministers at earlier ages
12. Increased ecumenical dimension, possibly moving toward mutual recognition of ministries

Diocesan Policy Towards a Working Ecclesiology

The following statements form the basis of an ecclesiology that allows the present parochial system to continue to function and to be able to receive new life and growth:[3]

1. No parish should be closed or consolidated with another parish simply because of a lack of ordained clergy. The only reason for closing or amalgamating parishes should come from a positive ecclesiology and theology of ministry.

2. Staffing in parishes should at least equal that of staffing when a number of priests was available for parish ministry. Thus, a parish which had a pastor and two full-time ordained associates ten years ago should have at least three full-time professional ministers on the staff at present.

3. The movement in a diocese should be towards smaller ecclesial communities where there is a real possibility of sharing faith and supporting one another in ministry, rather than

towards mega-parishes. Many parishes in the Catholic Church are, and have been for a long time, simply too large for effective pastoring. Churches of other ecclesial communities tend to have much smaller congregations and greater participation.

4. As the number of clerics diminishes, it is imperative that the bishop not try to use stopgap, potentially devastating short-term measures to fill the clerical vacancies. Such measures would include: assigning to parishes clergy with serious health problems, unduly delaying retirement age, and placing priests who have no talent as parish priests as leaders of community. Even the common practice of relying on "weekend helpers" (priests who come into parishes to say Mass on Sundays) might legitimately be questioned. In what way can someone who is in a parish only long enough to celebrate Mass really be the leader of the community?

Special Areas of Concern

As we continue to rethink our understandings of ministry, particularly Who is minister? and What is ministry itself? there are several areas of particular concern: the selection process for ministers; their formation and education; their ordination, institution, commissioning, or certifying; their evaluation, support, and rewards; and the role of women in the Church. This section will deal with these five areas first, with issues to be addressed, then with a "visioning" statement.

1. Selection Process

QUESTIONS TO BE ADDRESSED

Who is called to ministry? How are they called? Is the recruitment process in the diocese unified in its effort to "call forth" all ministries or is it still job-specific, i.e., priestly, religious, "other"? Is there long-term planning in the diocese about the future needs of all professional ministry or is it acting from crisis-to-crisis? What kind of discernment process is set up for potential ministers, both the young and the second-career people, to help them arrive at a realistic and practical decision concerning ministry?

VISIONING STATEMENT

The vocations office and the office of lay ministry in the future will be unified into one working organ to identify and develop *all* ministries and ministers in the Church, from the early process of discernment, through formation into ministry.

2. Formation and Education

QUESTIONS TO BE ADDRESSED

Is there only one real system of formation (for those who are to be ordained)? Are laity just plugged into this system but without having their own needs met in light of their not seeking (or being excluded from seeking) ordination? Can seminaries still continue to function and to adequately train men for ordained leadership roles without having laity, with whom they will work and among whom they will minister, involved on an equal basis? Are there institutions other than seminaries which are training lay ministers? Do the seminaries and other institutions work together with a common understanding of ministry and with the goal to train ministers in a comprehensive way, or is the training just haphazard? Is there any formation process for those not seeking ordination or not involved in religious life? (Can we just continue to hope that they will somehow evolve a good working spirituality on their own as they try to fit into a formerly exclusively celibate male system?) Is the diocese willing to assume some sort of financial assistance or support for those lay persons training for full-time Church ministry who do not plan on becoming clerics?

VISIONING STATEMENT

In the future the formation program in the diocese would seek to develop a plan to affirm the gifts and spiritual life of *all* seeking full-time ministry in the Church, so that their spiritualities, gifts, and needs are addressed to each individual. Trained together, sharing one another's lives, all ministers—lay and ordained, men and women, married and single—would learn during their formation to work together to build the Kingdom of God.

3. Ordaining, Instituting, Commissioning, Certifying

QUESTIONS TO BE ADDRESSED

Which official ministries are to be instituted, certified, commissioned? How are comprehensive ministries of "pastoral associate" and "lay pastor" going to be recognized and supported in parishes and in the diocese? Do these two ministries need to be certified and/or accredited? If so, what are the requirements for certification and how is the process to be set up? Are these ministries to the diocese? In what ways? Will these two ministries become hierarchical and clerical or, while maintaining professional competence, will they enhance the ministries of all the baptized? Will "lay pastors" be hired by local parishes with the approval of the bishop or will they go through the personnel board and direct appointment by the bishop? How will professional lay ministers relate to the permanent diaconate, both to the program and to deacons themselves? How will the pastoral associate and lay pastor relate to the clergy? Will they have voting rights or involvement in diocesan decision-making? If not, why not? If so, in what ways?

VISIONING STATEMENT

Ministries and understandings of ministry will continue to expand in the future. All ministers will be formed and educated together to recognize one another's gifts and give one another support. Lay ministers, while being professionally trained and competent, will be a sign to the whole Church of the seriousness of the call to baptismal ministry and the multiplicity of the gifts of the Holy Spirit.

4. Evaluation, Support, and Reward

QUESTIONS TO BE ADDRESSED

(1) *Job Security.* Will professional lay ministers receive a just wage, contract, health and retirement benefits, housing and car allowance, tenure, proper termination procedures, right to an advocacy process in disputes? Will there be unfair and discriminatory processes followed in competition with "reli-

gious" and the latter's need for less money? Will there be financial support shared by the diocese in a case where the parish cannot pay a just wage? Are there fair procedures for evaluation? (2) *Placement.* Will there be a diocesan placement file? Will the personnel board for priests also be responsible for advertising openings and helping place pastoral associates and lay pastors? Will there be the needed clarification of their relationship to the bishop in seeking placement and being canonically appointed? (3) *Professional recognition.* Are they accepted by clergy as fellow professionals? Do they share in decision-making on a diocesan level? Are they involved on diocesan committees involving ministry needs? Do they have opportunities for advancement? Do they have an adequate communication network? Do they have opportunities for ongoing education, for workshops, with finances and time allotted to them for yearly updates? (4) *Documents.* Will a manual be developed on pastoral associates and lay pastors regarding their rights and responsibilities and professional ethics? Are there liturgy documents being developed for lay presiding?

VISIONING STATEMENT

The diocese will take great care that all professional ministers, ordained and lay, work together as part of a ministry they share. Both ordained and lay ministers will be afforded opportunities to continue to develop their professional competence and keep current on the theology of the Church. They will all be involved in helping assess and respond to the ministry needs of the diocese.

5. *Women in the Church*

QUESTIONS TO BE ADDRESSED

Are we aware that the exclusion of women from ordained ministry is a discipline based on long-standing tradition in the Church, not on doctrine? That sexism has been condemned by the Church? That many women are being unjustly discriminated against even in non-ordained ministry? That we are called to the fullness of Christ through baptism, not to first-

and second-class citizenship based on gender? Is the diocese trying to recognize and eliminate gender-discrimination when not related to the issue of women's ordination? Are we aware that two of our sister Churches (who accept the same creeds and tradition), the Lutherans and Anglicans, now ordain women and that they have much practical experience and wisdom to share with us as we continue to examine the role of women in the Church? That the issue has not been dogmatically settled, although at present the magisterium has decided to continue the long-standing tradition of excluding women from priesthood?

VISIONING STATEMENT

For the present, recognizing both the gifts and the pain of women, we will do all that we can to end gender-discrimination in the Church in professional lay ministry and reaffirm the baptismal worth of women as equal to that of men. For the future, we will continue to examine the issues surrounding the ordination of women, both recognizing the past history of our own tradition and being prayerfully open to the promptings of the Spirit for new directions of ministry.

A Final Word

There is no way to recapture the pre-Vatican II Church, for our ecclesiology has moved beyond it. There is also no way to manufacture or "clone" enough ministers in the old mold to keep up with the growing needs of the Church and the dramatically and rapidly decreasing numbers of clergy. We can continue to deny these two facts—but only for a few more years. The "crisis" of dwindling numbers of ordained ministers is already upon us.

If we have the courage and faith, we can see this "crisis" as a God-given opportunity to explore and embrace our baptismal call to ministry and challenge ourselves to develop many more ways to live out this call to service. To not move, or to refuse to even see the need to move, leads to stagnation and death. To walk forward into the future of ministry, not knowing where we are going, is an act of supreme confidence in God. But the Holy Spirit has promised to be with us for all time. So let us step out, with fear perhaps but with certain faith, to see what the future will bring—and what *we* can bring to the future of our shared faith and vision.

Notes

1. Frank Sheedy, "Ask Me a Question," *Our Sunday Visitor*, October 28, 1984.

2. (New York: Newman, 1970), 73.

3. The first three statements were taken from a document entitled "Report to the Presbyteral Council from the Vicariate of Worship and Ministry," written by the vicar of worship and ministries for the archdiocese of Portland, Oregon, Fr. James Parker, and presented on April 4, 1985.

Bibliography

Bausch, William J. *The Christian Parish: Whispers of the Risen Christ.* Mystic, Conn.: Twenty-Third Publications, 1980.

__________. *Traditions Tensions Transitions in Ministry.* Mystic, Conn.: Twenty-Third Publications, 1982.

Bishops' Committee on the Liturgy. *Study Text 3: Ministries in the Church.* Washington: United States Catholic Conference, 1974.

Butt, Howard with Wright, Elliot. *At the Edge of Hope: Christian Laity in Paradox.* New York: Seabury Press, 1978.

Canon Law Society of America. *Code of Canon Law: Latin–English Edition.* Washington: Canon Law Society of America, 1983.

Coleman, William V., ed. *Parish Leadership Today.* West Mystic, Conn.: Twenty-Third Publications, 1979.

Doohan, Leonard. *The Lay-Centered Church: Theology and Spirituality.* Minneapolis: Winston Press, 1984.

Doyle, Thomas P. *Rights and Responsibilities: A Catholic's Guide to the New Code of Canon Law.* New York: Pueblo Publishing Co., 1983.

Fiorenza, Elisabeth Schussler. *Bread Not Stone: The Challenge of Feminist Biblical Interpretation.* Boston: Beacon Press, 1984.

__________. *In Memory of Her.* New York: Crossroad, 1984.

Flannery, Austin. *Vatican Council II: The Conciliar and Post Conciliar Documents,* vol. 1. Collegeville: The Liturgical Press, 1975.

Fox, Matthew. *Original Blessing: A Primer in Creation Spirituality.* Santa Fe: Bear and Co., 1983.

Geaney, Dennis. *Full Church Empty Rectory: Training Lay Ministers for Parishes Without Priests.* Notre Dame, Ind.: Fides/Claretian, 1980.

Haughton, Rosemary. *The Catholic Thing.* Springfield: Templegate Publishers, 1979.

Kelley, Kathleen E. *Through a Glass Darkly* (tape). Whitinsville, Mass.: Affirmation Books, 1982.

Kennedy, Eugene. *The Now and Future Church: The Psychology of Being an American Catholic.* Garden City, N.Y.: Doubleday and Co., Inc., 1984.

Nouwen, Henri. *Clowning in Rome.* Garden City, N.Y.: Image Books, 1979.

__________. *The Wounded Healer: Ministry in Contemporary Society.* Garden City, N.Y.: Doubleday and Co., Inc., 1972.

O'Dea, Barbara. *The Once and Future Church: Christian Initiation and Your Parish.* Kansas City: Celebration Books, 1980.

Power, David N. *Gifts that Differ: Lay Ministries Established and Unestablished.* New York: Pueblo Publishing Co., 1980.

Provost, James, ed. *Code, Community, Ministry: Selected Studies for the Parish Minister Introducing the Revised Code of Canon Law.* Washington: Canon Law Society of America, 1982.

Ruether, Rosemary Radford. *Sexism and God-Talk: Toward a Feminist Theology.* Boston: Beacon Press, 1983.

Sammon, Sean D. *Growing Pains in Ministry.* Whitinsville, Mass.: Affirmation Books, 1983.

Sanford, John A. *Ministry Burnout.* New York: Paulist Press, 1982.

Soelle, Dorothee, with Cloyes, Shirley A. *To Work and to Love: A Theology of Creation.* Philadelphia: Fortress Press, 1984.

Whitehead, Evelyn Eaton, and James D. *Christian Life Patterns: The Psychological Challenges and Religious Invitations of Adult Life.* Garden City, N.Y.: Image Books, 1982.

Zeis, Rita. *The Jonah Complex: Women and Fear of Responsibility.* Whitinsville, Mass.: Affirmation Books, 1983.

Appendix

Texts of Certain Canons

Canon 230

§1. Lay men who possess the age and qualifications determined by decree of the conference of bishops can be installed on a stable basis in the ministries of lector and acolyte in accord with the prescribed liturgical rite; the conferral of these ministries, however, does not confer on these lay men a right to obtain support or remuneration from the Church.

§2. Lay persons can fulfill the function of lector during liturgical actions by temporary deputation; likewise all lay persons can fulfill the functions of commentator or cantor or other functions, in accord with the norm of law.

§3. When the necessity of the Church warrants it and when ministers are lacking, lay persons, even if they are not lectors or acolytes, can also supply for certain of their offices, namely, to exercise the ministry of the word, to preside over liturgical prayers, to confer baptism, and to distribute Holy Communion in accord with the prescriptions of law.

Canon 517

§1. When circumstances require it, the pastoral care of a parish or of several parishes together can be entrusted to a team of several priests *in solidum* with the requirement, however, that one of them should be the moderator in exercising pastoral care, that is, he should direct their combined activity and answer for it to the bishop.

§2. If the diocesan bishop should decide that due to a dearth of priests a participation in the exercise of the pastoral care of a parish is to be entrusted to a deacon or to some other person who is not a priest or to a community of persons, he is to appoint some priest endowed with the powers and faculties of a pastor to supervise the pastoral care.

Canon 519

The pastor is the proper shepherd of the parish entrusted to him, exercising pastoral care in the community entrusted to him under the authority of the diocesan bishop in whose ministry of Christ he has been called to share; in accord with the norm of law he carries out for his community the duties of teaching, sanctifying and governing, with the cooperation of other presbyters or deacons and the assistance of lay members of the Christian faithful.

Canon 528

§1. The pastor is obliged to see to it that the word of God in its entirety is announced to those living in the parish; for this reason he is to see to it that the lay Christian faithful are instructed in the truths of the faith, especially through the homily which is to be given on Sundays and holy days of obligation and through the catechetical formation which he is to give; he is to foster works by which the spirit of the gospel, including issues involving social justice, is promoted; he is to take special care for the Catholic education of children and of young adults; he is to make every effort with the aid of the Christian faithful, to bring the gospel message also to those who have ceased practicing their religion or who do not profess the true faith.

§2. The pastor is to see to it that the Most Holy Eucharist is the center of the parish assembly of the faithful; he is to work to see to it that the Christian faithful are nourished through a devout celebration of the sacraments and especially that they frequently approach the sacrament of the Most Holy Eucharist and the sacrament of penance; he is likewise to endeavor that they are brought to the practice of family prayer as well as to a knowing and active participation in the sacred liturgy, which the pastor must supervise in his parish under the authority of the diocesan bishop, being vigilant lest any abuses creep in.

Canon 529

§1. In order to fulfill his office in earnest the pastor should strive to come to know the faithful who have been entrusted to his care; therefore he is to visit families, sharing the cares, worries, and especially the griefs of the faithful, strengthening them in the Lord, and correcting them prudently if they are wanting in certain areas; with a generous love he is to help the sick, particularly those close to death, refreshing them solicitously with the sacraments and commending their souls to God; he is to make a special effort to seek out the poor, the afflicted, the lonely, those exiled from their own land, and similarly those weighed down with special difficulties; he is also to labor diligently so that spouses and parents are supported in fulfilling their proper duties, and he is to foster growth in the Christian life within the family.

§2. The pastor is to acknowledge and promote the proper role which the lay members of the Christian faithful have in the Church's mission by fostering their associations for religious purposes; he is to cooperate with his own bishop and with the presbyterate of the diocese in working hard so that the faithful be concerned for parochial communion and that they realize that they are members both of the diocese and of the universal Church and participate in and support efforts to promote such communion.

Canon 759

In virtue of their baptism and confirmation lay members of the Christian faithful are witnesses to the gospel message by word and by example of a Christian life; they can also be called upon to cooperate with the bishop and presbyters in the exercise of the ministry of the word.

Canon 766

Lay persons can be admitted to preach in a church or oratory if it is necessary in certain circumstances or if it is useful in particular cases according to the prescriptions of the conference of bishops and with due regard for can. 767, §1.

Canon 767

§1. Among the forms of preaching the homily is preeminent; it is a part of the liturgy itself and is reserved to a priest or to a deacon; in the homily the mysteries of faith and the norms of Christian living are to be expounded from the sacred text throughout the course of the liturgical year.

§2. Whenever a congregation is present a homily is to be given at all Sunday Masses and at Masses celebrated on holy days of obligation; it cannot be omitted without a serious reason.

§3. If a sufficient number of people are present it is strongly recommended that a homily also be given at Masses celebrated during the week, especially during Advent or Lent or on the occasion of some feast day or time of mourning.

§4. It is the duty of the pastor or the rector of a church to see to it that these prescriptions are conscientiously observed.

Canon 861

§1. The ordinary minister of baptism is a bishop, presbyter or deacon, with due regard for the prescription of can. 530, n. 1.

§2. If the ordinary minister is absent or impeded, a catechist or other person deputed for this function by the local ordinary confers baptism licitly as does any person with the right intention in case of necessity; shepherds of souls, especially the pastor, are to be concerned that the faithful be instructed in the correct manner of baptizing.

Canon 911

§1. The pastor and parochial vicars, chaplains and for all who live in the house, the superior of the community in clerical religious institutes or societies of apostolic life have the right and the duty to bring the Most Holy Eucharist to the sick in the form of Viaticum.

§2. In case of necessity or with at least the presumed permission of the pastor, chaplain, or superior, who should later be notified, any priest or other minister of Holy Communion must do this.

Canon 943

The minister of exposition of the Most Holy Sacrament and the Eucharistic benediction is a priest or deacon; in particular circumstances the minister of exposition and reposition only, without benediction, is an acolyte, an extraordinary minister of Holy Communion or another person deputed by the local ordinary observing the prescriptions of the diocesan bishop.

Canon 1112

§1. With the prior favorable opinion of the conference of bishops and after the permission of the Holy See has been obtained, the diocesan bishop can delegate lay persons to assist at marriages where priests or deacons are lacking.

§2. A suitable lay person is to be chosen who is capable of giving instructions to those to be wed and qualified to perform the marriage liturgy correctly.